Praise for *Before the*

"Remi Kanazi is one of the most cou...
Before the Next Bomb Drops is a bea... ... urgent ...
freedom, justice, and resistance in every pocket of the world, from
occupied Palestine to gentrified Brooklyn. Read this book and prepare to
be inspired, enlightened, and emboldened."

—**Marc Lamont Hill**, CNN commentator
and host of HuffPost Live and *BET News*

"Here is how I consumed *Before the Next Bomb Drops*: I'd read a page,
then put it down, walk around the room for thirty seconds, then another
page followed by another mental health break, and then I'd repeat this
ritual. This book of poetry was devastating to pick up and impossible to
put down. Remi Kanazi has graced us with poems that are an antidote to
cynicism and a searing call of urgency for the human rights struggle of
our times. If you are immersed in the struggle for Palestinian lives, your
collection of literature is incomplete without this. But if you love poetry
and know nothing of the Middle East, I also could not recommend a
better book. Remi Kanazi has raised the bar for how art and politics can
serve one another for the greater good."

—**Dave Zirin**, the *Nation*

"This is by far Remi Kanazi's best and most mature work. It is also his
funniest, saddest, and most uplifting. His poems evoke places from
Brooklyn to Gaza, and he travels in time from 1948 to a present sometimes
experienced through images on a smartphone flitting past desensitized eyes.
Writing the lyrics of a movement, Kanazi aims upwards at the powerful and
inwards, challenging our own complacency. His rhymes and rhythms, filled
with sharp wit, irony, and deep empathy, are a great joy to read even as they
tackle some of the most urgent political struggles of our day."

—**Ali Abunimah**, cofounder of *Electronic Intifada*
and author of the *Battle for Justice in Palestine*

"Remi's verse is a series of indignant letters to the passersby of our historical
moment who thought they were minding their own business but who, in
fact, are perpetuating the problem with their privileged complicity. Each
verse made me sink deeper into my chair and helped unleash a cascade of
relieving tears: in anger, in mourning, and in hope."

—**Noura Erakat**, George Mason University and human rights attorney

"One picture is worth one thousand words they used to say with regard to Palestine and its suffering throughout the ages. This wonderful, elegant, and moving book will convince you that one poem is worth one thousand words and many pictures. It is a poetic, and very accessible, personal journey into the past and present of Palestine that will resonate with anyone concerned with the land and its people."

 —**Ilan Pappé**, bestselling author of the *Ethnic Cleansing of Palestine*

"Remi Kanazi asks whether his words 'hurt more than bombs dropped on Gaza?' They may not, but his words, which combine art with a burning desire to narrate, to shout, to shake, to shame and to humanize, create a lasting, almost self-regenerating mind image of the bombs dropped, the houses demolished and the communities uprooted. Kanazi's haunting poems are not written to be consumed; they reserve a place in one's conscience, in one's memory, and—hopefully—in one's praxis."

 —**Omar Barghouti**, Palestinian human rights activist
and cofounder of the BDS movement

Before the Next Bomb Drops

Rising Up from Brooklyn to Palestine

Remi Kanazi

Haymarket Books
Chicago, Illinois

Haymarket Books
P.O. Box 180165
Chicago, IL 60618
773-583-7884
info@haymarketbooks.org
www.haymarketbooks.org

ISBN: 978-160846-524-8

Trade distribution:
In the US, Consortium Book Sales and Distribution, www.cbsd.com
In the UK, Turnaround Publisher Services, www.turnaround-uk.com
In Canada, Publishers Group Canada, www.pgcbooks.ca
All other countries, Publishers Group Worldwide, www.pgw.com

Discounts on bulk purchases are available for organizations, teachers,
activists, and others. Please contact Haymarket Books for more information.

This book was published with the generous support of Lannan Foundation
and the Wallace Action Fund.

Cover design by Eric Ruder.

Printed in Canada by union labor.

Library of Congress CIP data is available.

10 9 8 7 6 5 4 3 2 1

To my mother, Libby
who instilled in me the confidence
to speak my mind and never back down
in the face of injustice

Contents

Acknowledgments

A number of brilliant writers, editors, and colleagues helped elevate the work before you and deserve mention. My sincere thanks go to Dao Tran and Ruth Goring, whose essential editorial guidance enhanced the poems in this collection. I remain indebted to Anthony Arnove, Jason Farbman, and the rest of the Haymarket Books team. My heartfelt appreciation goes to Lannan Foundation, which provided the perfect writing oasis to craft and shape the poems gathered here.

This book would not have taken flight without instrumental feedback supplied by Tahani Salah, Andrew Kadi, Achilles Yeldell, Jay Cassano, Rebecca Pierce, Carlo Vivenzio, Hannah Mermelstein, and Adam Smith.

My deepest gratitude goes to Yasmin Hamidi, who kept me level-headed throughout this entire process and offered invaluable editorial advice at every stage. Special mention to my siblings, Ramzi and Rania. They continue to challenge me as a poet and brother and have helped amplify my writing since the pen first hit the page.

There are countless authors, educators, and artists whose words and actions have inspired much of the poetry in this volume. From Edward Said, Angela Davis, and Michelle Alexander to Suheir Hammad, Amiri Baraka, and DAM to youth activists in Gaza, the West Bank, and Ferguson—for all these powerful voices, and so many more, I am thankful. Finally, this collection is a reflection of the work done by students, elders, and community organizers on Palestine and other critical issues globally. My work would not be possible without their tireless energy, their moving actions, and the path they continue to pave. The road is long, the challenges are many, but we have a fire inside of us that can't be extinguished.

Nakba

she was scared
seven months pregnant
guns pointed at temples
tears dropping
stomach cusped
back bent
dirt pathways
leading to
dispossession

rocking boats
waves crashing
people rushing
falling over each other
packing into small spaces
like memories

her home
   mandated
occupied
cleansed
conquered

terrorizers
sat on hills
sniping children
neighbors fled
on April 10
word came
of massacre

didn't fight
didn't leave
shells and bombs
bursting in air
like anthems

prayed for the dead
with priests and imams
prayed for the living
looking over shoulders
for the Irgun and Haganah

a warrior
raised life
planted trees
painted fruit
cared for the road
as if it was her garden

orphaned twice
after birth
from Palestine
whispered Yaffa
till final breath
never knew essence
until she found
emptiness

48 ways to flee
and she found Beirut
bullet holes in buildings

reminder of home
but not home

years later
daughters sat
on hills in the South
dreaming of breaking
water never touched

thinking of their mother
that warrior
how battles still
raged here and abroad

orchards flourished
propagandists called
them barren
land expropriated
for Europeans
thirsting for
territory

colonist
non-native
not from here
plant flags, call it home
rename cities and villages
uprooting graveyards
wiping/clearing/cleansing
memory that *this*
is not theirs

passed away
August 22, 2009
frail hands shook
lip trembled
didn't want to die
but suffered decades

she spoke in Arabic
broken English
wounded words
and murmurs
her eyes closed
but every so often
they blinked brilliance
memories that could not
be erased, uprooted
or cleansed

she had not forgotten
we have not forgotten
we will not forget
veins like roots
of olive trees

we will return
that is not a threat
not a wish
a hope
or a dream
but a promise

Lit Up

shells lit up the sky
like fireworks
breaking free darkness
as if awakening eyelids

her hazel bulbs staring up
to cascading snow showers
tiny hands wanting to touch
what she sees

in Iraq
they called it
Shake 'n Bake

in Gaza
no one even cared
to name it

on her skin
it was like
open flames
devouring
crisping flesh

deformed babies
crying out loud for help
a doctor cradling a child
falling apart in his hands

her stomach
     a cadaverous
          abyss

they are going to call him
          a liar
     a propagandist
   an apologist for terror

tell the world it wasn't
white phosphorous
claim elections
led to this disaster

they will open and close cases
the media blocks out
the blockaded
Mark Regev stands in
as if he works at CNN

this is not normal
not rational
but it is
and it was
and it won't stop being
just because you refuse
to acknowledge it

not enough space in a poem
to read all the names
of the dead

Zaid

   Hamza

      Shahad
Muhammad

pick   through   the damage
     shards
         of bone
     and ashes

every minute in anguish
every beat rips out
a father's breath

this is what you brought
what you laid bare
what you tried to wash away
what the media refuses to see
as the bomb's blast
shatters the rest of the dead
and terrorizes the living

it is
and it was
and it won't stop being
just   because   you   refuse
to   acknowledge it

Out of Season

you want peace between *our peoples*?
coiner of Demographic Threat
shrewd settlement builder
champion of the Nakba

you want us to get along
Mr. Nazareth Illit
shaving hilltops
like bad fades back
to 1970s South Africa

you want us to grin
cross legs and play
chess in the park
offer tea made from
poisoned water wells

Ma'ale Adumim
you were born in Moscow
in Tripoli, in San Francisco
chat me up at a checkpoint
before you realize I'm Palestinian

you stomp through destroyed villages
like Broadway dancers
build parks on cemeteries
and casually ask me
what my deal is

your furnace is heated with our wood
table covered with our cloths
figs plucked from our trees
and you want us to *coexist*?

I have no problem
with Palestinians
he says to me

squatter of colonies
usurper of aquifers
exploiter of occupied labor

there is Arabic on the awning
of the house you live in
no scars on palms
to show you built it

the stones you stand on
were laid by a grandfather
who passed away in 1997

> his daughter clutches a key older
> than any memory you possess
> presents a deed affirming your conquest

roughshod and ruthless
never even bothered
to change the locks

you want to sit
drink tea

and act *civilized*
in a park in Brooklyn
message me on Facebook
like we went to high school together
nonchalantly appeal to my *reason*

but your proverbs are out of season
anecdotes more played out
than tales of a land
without a people

your talking points don't resonate
your prime has passed
your legs are wobbling
the world is waking up
to this charade

you don't want peace
you want pieces
and this puzzle
doesn't end
well for
you

Until It Isn't

death becomes exciting
tolls, pictures, videos
tweeting carnage
instagramming collapse
hearts racing to break

24-hour entertainment
every glimpse, splinter
and particle of pain
jammed into torsos
and cheekbones

loved ones
want to sit
for a minute
and cry quietly

no words, no poetry
before Internet and
dialed-up emotions
before black and
white ideologies

before a person
      I called friend
      defended massacres
before the victims
      were laid to rest
before chemical weapons
      ravaged insides

before refugee
        meant grandmother

suffering 2.0
keyboard clicks
like bombs so effortlessly
            dropping

all damage collateral
never personal
voyeurs hop on and off
like carnival rides

death becomes
        exciting
until it isn't
until boredom sets in
and desensitization begins
until the next ride emerges
        somewhere else
        more captivating

Nothing to Worry About

the world is a messed-up place
rolled off your tongue
like an arrogant excuse

it's easy to say that
     when drone strikes aren't
leveling your block in Brooklyn
     when stop-and-frisk isn't
haunting your every move
     when your baby's
blood-spattered body isn't
plastered onto your
Park Slope avenue

Black men make up 40%
of the US prison population
nearly half for drugs that
white men abuse at a higher rate

drunk driving kills
more than crack
but DUIs don't attract
five-year sentences
don't see Jim Crow signage
in courtyards, but the same structures
still shackle the ankles of Black inmates

we spend
2.1 million dollars a year
to put a soldier in Afghanistan

35 thousand to lock a Black kid
up with racist laws
a third of that on education
and only 15 thousand dollars
on a minimum-wage job

pundits pontificate on
the color-blind era
we live in
where race gets
thrown out of the class
                              struggle
and intersecting systems
of oppression get no airtime

the world is a messed-up place
and you seem to be profiting nicely
noise-canceling headphones
blocking out ambulance and
police sirens in the faint distance

a Palestinian kid was shot in the back
the bullet subsidized by your tax dollars
the guy who used to deliver your weed
was just sentenced to eight years
in prison with no priors

the drone buzzing will be heard
one day over Brooklyn, but it will
skip your gentrified neighborhood
you have nothing to worry about
we don't want this *messed-up world*
to crash your baby's lullaby

An Empty Vessel

no more
gruesome images
   nails across faces
     generations collapsing
     on themselves

a father ripping through rubble
               coated in blood
     caved-in rooftops
immersed in the musk of death

no more cries
   crashing inside ears
   like cymbals
     can't unsee
     can't stop
     from happening

this is massacre
     Shejaiya is everywhere
this is annihilation
     infants in pieces
this is a war crime
     the beach is bleeding

she wants her husband back
     stop dehumanizing our men
she wants her best friend back
     stop killing our fathers

she wants her baby girl back
stop robbing our cribs

you incinerated classrooms
the morgues are overflowing
knew it was a shelter
white flags drenched in flesh
shelled the building again
children stuffed in ice cream freezers
knew what you were doing
the earth is still swallowing us

you are not the victim
not the narrator
don't get to tell us
how to process our pain

you are swindlers, terrorists
fascists fiending for our limbs
read the reports
become sick with yourself
you are everything
you levied against us

should be ashamed
Goliath on mass graves
yet you remain
an empty vessel
striding through a sea
of blood you spilled

This Poem Will Not
End Apartheid

this poem
will not end apartheid

my words, no matter how beautiful
clever or carefully strung together
will not end the occupation
allow the return of refugees
or create equality
within Israeli society

the status quo is a fantasy
telling us it's ok
to sit on our hands
call political art propaganda
rather than calling those
who politicize our lives
propagandists

every American
should ask this question
why are mortars and missiles
devastating open-air prisons
with money that should be paying
for our medical expenses?

to the academics
        and pseudo leftists
I appreciate your books
on Israeli massacres

but you refuse to take
bullets out of Israeli guns
with your stances

the problem is not just the occupation
or putting a better face on Zionism
because 750,000 Palestinians
        were displaced
before those settlements
        were constructed
half of them before
Israel was created

we don't need another book
explaining the situation
we need a lesson plan
to stop the next bomb
from dropping

silence is complicity
over-intellectualization tells us
to theorize on the power of art
while farmers are kicked off land
children are stoned
        on the way to school
people are caged in
        beaten and split
        from loved ones
blasted and broken
        in blockaded dungeons
bought and paid for
        with our tax dollars

we are part of the problem
that is not theoretical

    it is time
    to boycott *all*
    Israeli products
    and go to the root
    of the conflict

every 729
cultural institution
and dialogue farce
from Sabra to Ahava
Max Brenner to Aroma
Lev Leviev to SodaStream
switching drink preferences
stacks up little to 67 years
of continued dispossession

finally
to the artists
building bridges
between apartheid
and normalization
you serve an agenda
that rebrands colonialism
as enlightened liberalism
concerts, ballets, and raves
in Israel's Sun City
a haven and party stop
for pinkwashers
who callously ignore

Palestinian LGBTQ groups
working against all systems
of oppression

Palestinian civil society has spoken
don't cross this picket line
or cash in a paycheck
signed apartheid

cancel that gig
put down Stolen Beauty
and join the rest of us
on the right side of history

A Distraction

you weren't awake to notice
A Christmas Story marathon
played in the background
debates raged while Al Aqsa burned
history made as they flattened Gaza
stockings and stomachs stuffed
as politicians prepared mass graves
fit for children

you were camping
as the airport was struck
refilling lemonade in the backyard
while UN convoys were charred
counting down as they shelled
schools and mosques
in the swimming pool
as Sabra and Shatila
buried the dead

the radio wasn't on
the Celtics were playing
you were picking the kids
up from school
you were busy
flustered
working it out in therapy
fighting it out in your relationship
you were drunk in the East Village
you were consumed
we *all* are consumed

no fingers pointed
no blame placed on you
but the alarm clock is buzzing
if you are listening
if you are dreaming
if your nightmares
are flashing back
the alarm is sounding
it is time to wake up

#NoLessWorthy

they don't hate our way of life
      they despise our way of death
         granulated bones
         and crushed pelvises
            decimated
         decapitated
            even when
            you choose
            not to see it
      #WarOnTerror

✦

police pounded on his ribcage
like a new drum set, rammed their fists
into tendons and wounded limbs
boot marks on his face, eyes bruised shut
and busted lip, camera capturing every blow
too busy banging on his jawline to notice
#TariqAbuKhdeir

a smile
  a first kiss
    a ticket to college
    a life
no less worthy
than Natalee Holloway
or Casey Anthony's kid
      no *race war* in sight
just a one-way slaughter
and drubbing
    of Black existence
      #MikeBrown

✦

caged for 17 days
  deporter-in-chief
    gave no reprieve
     fracturing families
    by the millions
   seven years stateside
shipped away
like airport luggage
  #undocumented

arms raised
        waving back
and forth
        at the sky
        like windshield
        wipers
        in a rainstorm

soldier didn't blink, opened fire
man collapsed on himself
like a building demolition
#Baghdad

✦

you don't deserve a medal for speaking up
against misogyny, finger snaps for railing
against the prison industrial complex
special hugs for standing with
undocumented communities
combating oppression isn't
a game you get prizes for
#solidarity

Dislocation

peace is a lucrative industry
  an engine
    a profit model
      a 501c3
built on consumer confidence
      and shrewd
        business practices

30% of the Palestinian Authority
        budget is for *security*
subcontracting occupation
      and expanding jails
        across the West Bank

while fishermen are shot at sea
Haifa, Yaffa, and the Galilee
transfer to Ramallah and Gaza City
Jerusalem is swapped out for Abu Dis
Palestine becomes
           22%
      15%
10%
the Jordan Valley
morphs into a military zone
orchards become E-1
split blocks, and settler roads
rocks become terror
wombs become threats
return becomes national suicide

and millions of Palestinians
are left hanging in exile
    diaspora becomes foreign
Lebanon, Jordan, Syria, Iraq
Egypt, Chicago, Santiago
anywhere but home

we are always the problem
clothes hung out to dry
    everyone writes a poem
we have been reduced to odes
and books and a class and a clash
at a NYU bar with two sides
and intractable struggle

we've been separated
compartmentalized, carved
up and spit out by processes

and we are told
theft is peace
ethnocracy is democracy
dispossession is liberation
anything to numb the world
to this dystopian reality

Hebron

this once bustling street
now a ghost town
scattered with the remnants
of Palestinian shops
rusted awnings
and green doors
welded shut

gas the Arabs scrawled across entryways
gas the Arabs inscribed by a people
who have been gassed before
children trounced, water wells poisoned
water tanks shot, sewage heaved
upon mothers

usurpers parade around
razing whatever is in their sight

American-born settler
butchered 29 Palestinians
as they prayed in Ibrahimi mosque

clip after clip unleashed
like a bad action flick
extra ammo to catch injured
worshipers crawling away

Zionism's wonder boy
hailed as a hero

a shrine erected
in his name

Israeli soldiers on the scene
lashed out at victims, beat protesters
jailed community members
and executed blood donors
for pebbles thrown against
a fortress of occupiers

Oslo doves used the mosque's
blood-soaked carpet to tear
the city in two
colonize the Cave of the Patriarchs
and asphyxiate the local economy
salt in the wound and a thumb
in the eye of loved ones mourning

850 settlers strangling the lives
of 30,000 Palestinians
apartheid on full display
the Western media
on a coffee break

no *rising tensions*
no *breakdown in peace*
because the brutalized
and dead aren't Jewish

20 years later
young boys are still
being stuffed into prison

collective punishment
the national mantra
Shuhada Street
remains closed
a people
remain deprived

but a simmering is taking place
it isn't a newspaper headline
or talk of a third intifada
but an acknowledgment
inside their bones
this wretched nightmare
is merely a moment in time

Normalize This!

Nor·mal·i·za·tion applies to relationships that convey a misleading or deceptive image of normalcy, symmetry or parity, despite a patently abnormal and asymmetric relationship of colonial oppression and apartheid.
—Palestinian Campaign for the Academic and Cultural Boycott of Israel

nothing
is normal
about occupation

nothing normal about
apartheid, ethnic cleansing
siege, blockade, Israeli-only roads
the bombing of water wells, schools
mosques, and UN buildings

nothing normal
about putting a civilian
population on a diet
paying nonindigenous
colonizers
to occupy land
that is already inhabited

rewriting the Nakba
with each stolen childhood
trying to desensitize the bullet holes
and claw marks put into the bodies
of Bassem Abu Rahme and Rachel Corrie

no
I don't want to normalize with you
I don't want to hug, have coffee
talk it out, break bread
sit around the campfire
eat s'mores and gush about
how we're all the same

I don't want to share the stage
cowrite a poem
submit to your anthology
talk about how art
instead of *justice*
can forge a better path

I don't want to indulge
          your amnesia
          about a glorious past
have a therapy session
          on two sides
          with equal grievances

the only thing barren
is your moral capacity
blooming a settler colonial state
with appropriated culture

I will not fight for your privilege
nor will I seek to normalize it

your dialogue group
is a breeding ground for injustice

just look at the board members
and the ZOA sponsorship

Zionism is the real
demographic threat
infecting the minds
of millions with racism
they were hooded in the South
pushing darker nations into Bantustans
jailing young men in H Blocks
in North Ireland

in case you missed the hint
I don't want to pretend all is ok
that bombs dropped on Gaza
don't have a manufacturer
the pilot doesn't have a nationality
or Shimon Peres is any better
than Avigdor Lieberman

it's not *just* the occupation
            stupid
it's the right of return
equality for all Palestinians
it's the transformation
from an exclusivist
supremacist state
to a nation
for all of its citizens

you deserve *nothing*
more than equality

which means more than
African refugees are provided
in South Tel Aviv

you are the shining light
on a settlement hill
reminding the world
that racism often comes
in nice packaging

we don't give the Sudan
3.4 billion dollars a year
in military aid
don't have preferential trade
agreements with North Korea
don't call Iran a democracy

you are a proxy for empire
a 1950s ethnocracy trapped
in 21st-century clothing

yes, Israel
you are singled out
with aid, weapons, and
UN vetoes in your favor

did I hurt your feelings?
should we hug after the show?
do these words hurt more than
bombs dropped on Gaza?
white phosphorus incinerating
the insides of children?

I am not the bad guy
you are defending
the bad system
your words
and actions
have consequences

you are either
with oppression
or against it
I didn't write history
and didn't choose for you
to stand on the wrong side of it

your system of injustice
is coming to an end
and whether you
recognize it or not yet
it will be liberating
for you too

Anything But Iraq

That's it, the war is over.
—A US soldier to NBC's Richard Engel
(December 17, 2011)

I.

the war on Iraq is over
don't see the mass graves
       the coffin boxes
       the cancer rates in Fallujah
there are no winners or losers

no need for electricity
       water and
       sewage facilities
because
we have
       expanded weapons deals
       the world's biggest embassies
       and Americans filling streets
       with contractors armed to the teeth

wherever there's America
       there's *democracy*
       creating Green Zones and
       hired guns who come back
       with PTSD and vacant souls

patriots call it liberation
the bombed call it imperialism
empire, desire for resources

the problem is Afghanistan
                I mean Iraq
            I mean Afghanistan
                no, Pakistan, Yemen
              Somalia, Iran
          our ally Saudi Arabia
                it's Al Qaeda on Mars
            the Taliban from the moon

it's security
        domestic, global
        democracy building
        leveling villages
        to protect civilians

we are brave
wear armor
call people heroes
        give them names
                faces
                and favorite colors
but don't even mention
the Brown ones over there
        whose graves we barely
        fit into statistics
never mind lives
with vivid memories

II.

Merriam-Webster: Iraq. *noun*
1. a war America fought under false pretenses
2. an unaccomplished mission
3. an object we reference on anniversaries
4. an investment that didn't yield the expected benefits
5. in the past; not to be thought about or discussed

III.

Iraq is destroyed
a nation became a broken item bought
a sectarian land, a money suck
a place where soldiers die
a mistake, anything but Iraq
anything but a place with history
and textures and complexities
and a culture, a place that remains
no matter how hard you strike it
no matter how many times you
bend the spine of its letters
you cannot break it

you, who worship
the tank shell and sound bite
take Iraq out of your mouth
let a people breathe
for just one moment
without trying to
set it ablaze

Tree-Lined Empire

4 a.m. on a tree-lined block in Brooklyn
million-dollar brownstones lined up
like Monopoly properties
a homeless man in his 50s
travels from apartment
to apartment collecting bottles

good evening, he nods
as our paths begin to intersect
tree-lined empire, streamlined stereotypes
drunk, lazy, blaming-the-victim culture
collecting bottles, hard at work
digging through trash cans

give / don't give becomes debate
over $4.50 coffee, an inebriated friend you are
walking with bestows conventional wisdom
he's probably going to use the money
for drugs or alcohol

rarely do people
who have never been without
shelter or luxury focus on action
homelessness created by capitalism
settler colonialism, the thirst for more
of what isn't yours

exchanged words
gave the man some money

not to end poverty, supplant strategy
or replace structural analysis
but because I live in a country
where there are three times as many
empty homes as there are homeless people
where patients die without health care
enough hospitals, beds, machines, nurses
doctors, and people get sick, go bankrupt
while resources remain in abundance

no discussion on gutting mental health
lost minimum-wage jobs, and PTSD
overrepresentation of Black
and Native communities
on US streets

affordable housing, a talking point
substance abuse criminalized
poverty needs bootstraps
put guns in 19-year-old hands
send them off to wars for profit
but step over veterans begging
for change outside Rite Aid

so righteous is this
richest nation in the world
built on genocide and slave labor

what does it say when a man
digging through the trash
represents the problem

when his situation is merely
an indictment of the foundation
this society rests upon

An Open Letter
to Campus Zionist Groups
and University Chancellors

this conversation is a dialogue
   my Facebook post
   that comment back
   the e-mail chain
   the article
    and response to the article
   the soon-to-be Q&A
   the debate in the quad
   yesterday's phone call
   that time I smiled
    said hello
    and held the door
    for a member
    of Bruins for Israel

you know where we can't
have any kind of dialogue?
in Palestine

because I'm not allowed to return
because dispossessed Palestinians
    aren't allowed to return
because indigenous refugees returning
    would put ethno-religious
    supremacy in jeopardy

it's easy to whine
about your comfort level
when there isn't a checkpoint
stopping us from meeting

no wall blocking tonight's
event from happening

I don't get to drop
white phosphorus
on your dorm room
and call it security
if our chat doesn't go well

so let's have a thought
experiment on *tolerance*

would Hillel, J Street
and university Zionist groups
come to a meeting to dialogue
on whether or not Jews should
have equal rights in America?

whether or not Jews
should face checkpoints
on campus in America?

whether or not Jews should be
stuffed into open-air prisons
in America?

yet you *expect* Palestinians
to indulge your *racism*?

that is not dialogue
that is not moving forward
that is the status quo
that is the bomb's blast
that is the silence
of solitary confinement

you want to hug over justice
I'll stretch my arms
and fingertips so wide
my knees buckle

but I saw you read
a prepared question
off your android
given talking points
by StandWithUs
to derail the discussion

      you don't want dialogue
      you want domination
      and that is not something
      I can offer you

most administrations don't care
about *campus climate*
they care about donors
and empty e-mail boxes
houses made of sand

willing to crumble
at the first sight of rain

overbloated salaries and egos
overanxious trigger fingers
willing to throw as many
Black and Brown bodies
under the bus as need be

so chancellor X
   challenge us
student council Y
   let your backbone fold on itself
administrator Z
   tell me about climate
   while artillery shells
   eviscerate natives
   you never cared
   to learn about

because students are coming
and they aren't stopping
          cowering
          caving
to veiled threats, stripped funding
and attacks on their organizations

you made a miscalculation
   the road to freedom
   is not through the academy
but these students
   armed with more passion

than donor funds lining
   your pockets
are sure as hell
going to smash
your roadblocks

This Divestment Bill
Hurts My Feelings

this divestment bill
hurts my feelings

that Caterpillar bulldozer *ended life*
in the body of an American citizen
drove her bones into the ground
while a company cashed in
on the sale

the claws of D-9 bulldozers
unearth the livelihood
of occupied Palestinians
uprooting their graveyards
to make way
for illegal settlements

but we need
a positive
campus climate

while HP's stock rises on division
producing technology
to segregate Palestinians
biometric IDs at checkpoints
enhancing the naval blockade
of an open-air prison

Palestinians on campus
listen to words like *climate*

positive, hurt feelings
knowing their tuition
invests in companies
raining terror on loved ones

that suffering
  like their voices
is nonexistent
to student board members
looking for cushy jobs
at top-five law firms

but this divestment bill
    it's DIVISIVE!

the Montgomery bus boycott: divisive
the grape boycott: one-sided
abolishing slavery: radical
Nelson Mandela: a terrorist
indigenous: savages
women's suffrage: complicated
desegregation: provocative
Hiroshima: security
internment camps: a necessity
Bantustans: autonomy
Iraq: liberation
Palestine: barren

        there is always an excuse

catch phrases, talking points
strip away names and faces

we are being militant, unreasonable
there is context to this oppression

the word *apartheid*
makes you feel *uncomfortable?*

it's apartheid by definition
fits the '73 convention
by law
it is a crime
against humanity

two sets of laws
for two people
labor, land ownership
access to education

50 laws of discrimination
67 years of colonization
27,000 homes demolished
nearly a million arrested
since '67

whoa, whoa, whoa!
no one said Israel
doesn't have problems
but why the singling out
on campuses?

you mean like
Darfur, Tibet, South Africa
sweatshops, Coca-Cola

animal testing
the Keystone Pipeline
undocumented rights
the prison industrial complex
fossil fuels, teachers' unions
university cuts and bottled water?

   the real question
   why are you singling out
   any injustice for protection?

let me get the next one for you
Israel is democratic

democratic like coal is clean
Miller Lite is the same
great taste, less filling
and McDonald's salads
are healthy

these are not
imagined scenarios
our tuition dollars
are profiting from death
divestment is the next step

this is not about
a nation or a people
but what is being done
to people
in our names
with our currency

this university
will not liberate anyone
but it can choose to cease
making a buck off misery

vote YES for divestment
NO to appeasement

affirming injustice
isn't positive
for any climate

#WhatRemains

a laboratory
testing ground
coated metal canisters
and cracked limbs
creating new markets
with each bone broken
#NabiSaleh

✦

still wets the bed
shivers in the corner
the last clean sheet
around his shoulders
embarrassed   afraid
            stares out
        the window
teeth chattering
the buzzing
unyielding
        #OccupiedSky

split chest open
  blood-soaked fabric
  hung off his limp body
    wide-eyed grin
    marching with children
    raising fists at US claws
    digging up history
tear gas canister
broke the portrait
robbed his life
    and left anguish
    on his doorstep. #Bilin

✦

Palestine is not Ferguson
not South Africa, not Jim Crow
not Emmett Till, not an earthquake
tsunami, the Holocaust, death cabs in Chile
it is not everything, but it is so much of
something

my heart breaks for Mike Brown's family
spine jerks at mention of a shotgun shell
entering Renisha McBride's body
a knot in my throat wrenches
at Black bodies on pavement

it is not the same, but the swollen eyes
the stuttering breath, the anger rushing
through the corridors of our bones feels
so familiar. #Palestine2Ferguson

cooking in the kitchen
  sfiha in the oven
      greens laid out
      on the counter
              artillery shelled
        mangled body parts
    scattered limbs
  and severed head
couldn't identify
what remained
  wedding finger
  still intact
child wailing
in the next room
  #Gaza

Solidarity

I.

you can speak
you always do
never minded replacing
indigenous syllables
with Western vernacular
politics on paper
but never in practice
cleansed native tongues
on soapboxes built on
stolen land

we would no longer smile
hold the door, take your coat
get on our knees and praise
this fool's gold

not palatable
not reasonable
never white enough
narratives ghostwritten
poorly and without
our permission

I am not looking for you
academic savior
know-it-all solidarity activist
condescending anti-Zionist
owe you nothing for introspection

will award you no medal as you shout
your own name at the top of your lungs

Palestinian women worked decades in camps
weaving fabric until fingers bled
watched their children die
as they built foundation for return

their names have never been mentioned
faces put on a poster or hailed as heroes
they built classrooms because their hearts
willed it, memory could not erase it

II.

when we make saviors out of movements
organize around egos and forgo campaigns
pedestals and ivory towers must be critiqued
your contribution is just that, a contribution

I wake thankful
for those who speak out
refuse, resist
but solidarity
comes with recognizing
and checking privilege

solidarity comes with knowing
that you are not better than others
simply because you hold a mic
students are not worker bees
while you take all the credit

Palestinians are not victims
that need to be saved
children that need to be dictated to
solidarity is not a golden pass
to stomp, abuse, and run over
you want to battle oppression?
confront your own complicity
in communities of solidarity

Appetite for Appropriation

Arab is the new Black
a speaker says
to a nodding crowd

he's being profound
making comparisons
we are *the new oppressed*
45 million baton-passers
traversed a turbulent history
now living post-racially
in Obama's America

tell that to millions
stopped and frisked

tell that to Black graduates
who see double the average
unemployment rate post-graduation

tell that to legislators
    implementing racist drug laws
supporting mandatory minimums
    that fill their private prisons

tell that to the mothers
of Sean Bell, Rekia Boyd
Jordan Davis and Aiyana Jones

tell that to those whose executed loved ones
can't fit between the rigid letters
of this stanza

don't need to go overseas
to see militarism at play
don't need to bomb Baghdad
to witness *shock and awe*
go to Shaw, to Philly, to Harlem
catch the tears of Ramarley Graham's father
before they crash to the floor

we have to think critically
address structurally and
not replicate the processes
of appropriation our own
communities condemn in society

rush to chide hummus being labeled Israeli
but use Black history as garnish
in our struggle for liberation
non-Black communities of color
don't get a pass to promote
problematic politics for elevation

Black lives aren't a punch line
Black Lives Matter isn't a slogan
Black suffering isn't a tool to fight
another community's persecution

if to prop up your own plight
you have to shove another

people's face down in the mud
you are simply affirming
the very structure of cruelty
you claim to be combating

Refugee

I.

she has never
seen the sea

sunlight imprinted
on her father's skin
waves crashing
at his feet
smile tattooed
underneath boyish grin
snapping pictures
with closing eyelids

her father's face
flush on recollection
the same waves that had
clenched like an angry jaw
as his mother pushed him
forward like a train car

watched his neighbor drown
tears streaming
eyes connecting
screams muffled
as inhalation
suffocated lungs

muscles weary
skin pruning

barely a boy
knowing he would
never return

his neighbor
   an older man
born in Akka
looked dapper
at dinner parties
looked helpless that day
   his body revolting
   against death
a pool intent
on swallowing him

so many stroking
to get on boats departing
who'd have known this gulf
would be their deathbed

II.

she has been beaten
ID checked
body thrown to the ground
fists and feet pummeled
fractured hip, shoulder broken
heart, too many times

tear gas inscribed on her lungs
she wrote back on her breath
that the canister's defeat is near

III.

these fields are ours
she told me

before the Europeans
   and Brooklynites
before the swimming pools
   army jeeps and barbed wire
before the talks, roadmaps
   and Swiss cheese plans
before declarations rewrote history
   those hills met footprints
   and that can't be erased

like village massacres
   can't be erased
like *broken bones* policies
   can't be erased
like the screams ringing
   in her father's ears
   can't be erased

we are the boat
   returning to dock
we are the footprints
   on the northern trail
we are the iron
   coloring the soil
we cannot
   be erased

Refuse

don't pull that trigger
you don't have to go
don't have to fight
conquer, kill, beat
torture, scar

your own conscience
will eat away at you
remind you, tell you
what you did
at night in hallucinations
broken sleep and deep sweats
in shattered relationships
and black eyes
it is not business
as usual

you will climb that chair
creep up that ladder
put a rope around your neck
and leap to go back
to the way it was
swallow a shotgun
it will fester
jolt and choke you

those who sent you
won't remember
won't care, won't treat
won't keep promises

you will die alone
even if surrounded
by loved ones

don't pull that trigger
step off that ledge
you are not
jumping alone
pull back
lift that finger
turn in the other direction

there will be repercussions
but they cannot last forever
that will last forever
that gunshot
that trigger pulled
  will not end
  be amended
  be fixed
when you come back
a shell of your former self

refuse to be damaged
refuse to be pawned
refuse to serve
their agenda

you have a choice
remember that
you can
refuse

Sumoud

I.

Ahmed was four years old
the first time his father
was torn away from him

wasn't afraid of ghouls
under his bed
or the grim reaper
in his closet

the nightmare
hovered over him
thermal night-vision goggles
and loaded M16s
plowing through the house
searching for their target

he could see their breath
in the cold night
feel their spit
on his warm skin
the front door
kicked in at 3 a.m.

Yallah! shouted in Hebrew accents
other words and phrases
he couldn't understand

his mother
belting out futile tones
    an umbrella
facing a tsunami

Ahmed's father
taken for 94 days
a constellation
of blue and purple
bruises across
his dilapidated frame
no charge, no trial
no lawyer present

his family has accounts
and statistics, broken limbs
and cracked ribs
but the puffed cheeks
from tattooed tears
tell more stories
than words can hold

every neighborhood affected
every city pillaged of men
administrative detention
begins and never ends

II.

studying abroad
father caged at home
divest! roars from his diaphragm

he builds mock checkpoints
erects wall panels so students
can witness a hint
of his existence

Ahmed's father remains
under administrative detention
    no convenient resolution
    to end this poem with
        no Facebook status
        tweet or Instagram post
        to unclasp shackles

thousands went on hunger strike
and will again, until walls crumble
prisons fall and something arises
out of the ashes of this misery

and on that day, we will write
and scream and dabke in squares
and race to rooftops and celebrate
what this world can bring
if we push it to the brink

right now a young man
is without a father
that bellowing laugh
that joyous grin
that warm embrace

his hero
who starved himself
to raise a mirror
up to the world
once again

Say Their Names

I.

terrorist, savage, Islamofascist
      create boxes to put Muslim men in
ghetto, thug, gangbanger
      create cages to surround Black men with
hero, liberator, savior
      create pedestals to put occupiers on

II.

               life taker
            bomb dropper
            back breaker
            cut, dice, smash
            kick, squeeze, knead
            strip families

trash, slash
      piss on Korans
stress, twist
      put
        on
      knees
locked, shocked
      waterboarded up
killed men
      pumped fists
      waved flags

burned bodies
buried bodies
repeat cycle

III.

NATO militants
drone murder daily
dropping broken consciences
on villages
filled with civilians

Americans shopping

corpses littered
with shrapnel
spread   like
Christmas   dinner

IV.

42 Yemenis

cruising missiles

Abudallah
Saleha
Ibrahim
Asmaa
Salma
Fatima
Sumia

                              37
                       30
              13
                     9
                              4
                     3
              1

                              father
                     wife
                       son
daughter
                              daughter
daughter
                              daughter

          say their names
like Newtown children
          say their names
al Bayda, Shejaiya
Chicago, Staten Island
          say their names
like haunting whispers
          say their names
so we
never repeat
never lash out again
never forget the boxes
the innocent have been
put in

#InsideOut

building bombed, beams through flesh
      buried under rubble
      suffocated to death
but only beheading is barbaric to the West
      #Gaza

✦

a smashed window always rings louder
in the media's ears than the clacking
of six rounds emptied into
a Black teen's body
#Ferguson

✦

beat so bad her
insides went silent
Muslim, covered
   with blood
            no
love or light found
on this Parisian block
#HateCrime

45 degrees
clear to the sky
still would terrorize
soldiers and police aim for the head
chest. kneecaps. ligaments. debilitate. disable
bilin. nabi saleh. oakland. athens. #teargas

✦

first date
dad's cologne
scenting his skin
heart beating fast
house in the distance
stopped   frisked   groped

routine checkpoint
blue bruises   white cops
protect quotas   serve the system
dealers of discrimination in uniform
#StopAndFrisk

1000-pound
  bombs
don't inquire about
the sexuality
      of victims below
#pinkwashing

✦

repackaged racism and domination
of natives may mask the messenger
but it doesn't transform the parcel
#LiberalZionism

✦

transphobic feminists   misogynistic socialists
anti-Black leftists   ableist Palestine activists
selective justice   isn't a path to liberation
#NotJustUs

Mourning in Cairo

what is life
when shoes
         are made
of cinderblocks?

when elbows
and eyelids
pull to the
         ground
like gravity
is collecting
a debt

silence is suffocating
sleep unsettling
movement rigid
haunting memories
of what was
and isn't anymore

never imagined
that phone call
never played out
the conversation
or lack of conversation

knees buckling
stomach dropping
beads of sweat

racing down
his forehead

fumbling with keys
panic after panic
eyes darting back
and forth, crooked
      picture
    framing
  their
  embrace

he stumbled
into the mosque
shirt untucked
hands shaking
senses overcome
by the stench of death

couldn't process
mothers tearing
at faces and chests
broken-down neighbors
assaulted by anguish

white shrouds covering
rows of wrapped bodies
one
    after
        another
forced to identify his kin

what was left after the bullets
got through with him

he slowly lay down
curled into a ball beside his boy
hoping to hear one word
feel one heartbeat
                    and began
to whisper:
                    I am here
                    I am here now
                    I am not going anywhere
                    I am the wound
                    inside your flesh

Goldstone

a wanton act
deliberate and premeditated
raw sewage lagoons struck
broader pattern of destruction
not justified by military necessity
this mission concludes

report read like poetry
  the drumbeat
  of war crimes
human shields
armed forces behind
the practice has (not)
been discontinued

called you a traitor
self-hater
Jew-basher
anti-Israel Nazi
scumbag
aide of terror

  called yourself
a Zionist

crumbled
under criticism
not a jurist
    a plagiarist
of weakened will

one small issue
1,400 problems
too many survivors
Samouni family testimony
huddled on instruction
   died one by one
   as shells hit buildings
   concrete slabs smothering
   trapped relatives

you became
the report
so they could
shell you too

don't need Goldstone
not one glimmer of light
needs to be taken off
the smiling faces who rebuild
what you tried to demolish
in the *Washington Post*
and *New York Times*

the scars don't go away
the bomb blasts
are never taken back
when the smoke clears
history will shine on
where you stood
what deals you made
whose lives you brokered

you will be remembered
an empty shell
rewriting reality to fit
an acceptable narrative

Tone It Down

you should be funny on stage
tell jokes, soften your message
everyone likes humor

you're normal in conversation
but your poems are so . . . angry

angry?
       (breathe)
slow down
don't cause a scene
       cut to platitudes
neatly fit packages
of entertainment
to make him laugh

  hahahahaha
Barack Obama
just murdered
a wedding party
full of Muslims

  hahahahaha
that mother
hunched over her son's
dismembered body in Gaza
   tore   divots
   into her skin
just so she could feel life again

let me put on
a clown costume
   sit you on my knee
   and tell you a story
one that you could
never relate to
   because your family
   never went through it

once upon a time . . .
      during the ethnic cleansing
         of Palestine

once upon a time . . .
      birth defects went up
         500% in Fallujah

once upon a time . . .
      they beat his body so badly
         he bled internally
            carved *raghead*
            into his bare thigh
            and pissed on his
            lacerated limbs

      you said nothing
      did *nothing*

is that what you
want me to say?
that you place so little
value

on human life
that I need to put on
a clown costume
to entertain you?

let you know
how this country was founded
who it was founded for
and how we both still benefit
from that privilege?

no, that's not what you want
you want a funny story
so here's one:

> taxpayer
> 1,000-pound dollar signs
> drop
> on eight-story buildings

reservations aren't something
you make before dinner

> leaflets littering the sky
> mean you may be
> grieving relatives
> by morning

here's another scream:

> artillery shells
> bury humans alive

refugees die in camps
they were pushed into

grandmothers can still
feel the rigid earth
that dug into their feet
as they scrambled north

does that make you feel *uncomfortable?*
like cluster bombs stealing the legs
of children in South Lebanon?

how much strength does it take
to climb atop the world
and not give a damn?

no, guy that came up to me after the show
and asked me why I couldn't be more like
the apolitical Jewish comic
that came on after me

no, I can't be that guy
                    and *no*
you wouldn't be asking me this question
if half your family drowned
rushing to get on boats
as people fired from behind

this is not a poem
this is a reminder
to all sloppy critics

who come up to me
after a show

slavery isn't funny
> *feminism isn't angry*
and the dumb crap
> *that comes out of your mouth*
> > *isn't ok*
> *just cuz you end it with a smile*

> but if you are really
> in the mood for critique

> do yourself a favor
> > *look inward*
> keep that finger pointed
> and work on your own shit

because I would rather be labeled
> an angry Brown poet
than be an apathetic American
who turned away just long enough
to never actually have to give a damn

Peace Process

we are told to come to the table
no chair, no utensils, no napkin
designated for us

we are told of a feast
but we are not eating
have not tasted flesh
only crumbs that fell
as the biscuits
were gorged

we are told that after dinner
we will tango, but our ankles
have been shackled
and we have no room to move

we are told
that we will meet a broker
but this dinner party is full
only friends remain
and we have been culled
as festive game

The Grin behind the Tears

the first time Samir
was arrested
he was 14

he tells stories more vivid
than movie screens
syllables like paintbrush
strokes on empty canvases
pulls you in deeper
with shifting intonations

rattles off torture like a shopping list
fists and spit to the face
naked body threatened with rape
face submerged under water
tied up and beaten
electric shocks to the body
thinking death is imminent
sleep deprivation, music pulsating
isolation regular, stress positions always
blindfolded and battered, bound to a chair
knocked over and punched unconscious
wakes chained, beaten again

lifts up his shirt: calves to stomach
to shoulders a human rights report
considers himself lucky, sordid stories
of sexual abuse, objects used

no prosecution
no policies ended
no one steps in to stop it
the warden is the judge, the civilian
the settler, the politician, the police chief
there is no law under occupation

Samir works with children
reading stories, leading workshops
mapping programs, always teaching
always building

he says to me:

>*no matter how tight Israel thinks its grip is*
>*the bullets, the bombs, the checkpoints*
>*the UN vetoes, the congressional applause*
>*these children are more powerful than F-16s*
>*more assured than US military aid*
>
>*they will climb walls, skirt roadblocks, dodge tear gas*
>*they will unravel injustice by their very existence*
>*in every breath they take, every wedding that's held*
>*every newborn they bring into this world, they know it*
>*Zionists know it, the occupation's days are numbered*

Bobby

They have nothing in their whole imperial arsenal
that can break the spirit of one Irishman
who doesn't want to be broken.
—Bobby Sands

always cold
blue bruised feet
and scarred back

shivering hands
grabbed for more material
barely draping thinned-out shoulders

crows staggered outside prison bars
nourished on maggots you threw
broken but never broken

so many hands coming at you
you didn't know what was baton
and what was fist

a terrorist
stripped rights, beatings
blocked-out letters, screened visits
inhumanity seeped through
your letters on toilet paper

they stole from you daily
clattering keys, voices
of A, B, C in the distance

as you peered through
a slender crevice
to warn others

died three years later
on hunger strike
insides deprived
conscience replenished

the new empire
gave you no proper eulogy
terrorists can never be harmonized
not until the graves are filled
and liberation is long past

we too would fight our own
war on terror across a dozen nations
tearing apart citizens at home
and stuffing them into H Blocks
in Cuba, downtown Manhattan
internment facilities
secret black sites from
Lithuania to Thailand

what we learn from history
is to repeat it, build upon its cruelty
shape and tailor its brutality
for new systems

Bobby's body
buried like many others
    not just a mural

or poster or reference
a voice lifting up souls
freezing, tired, hungry
in cold dark cells

but not broken
even in death, not broken

they could build a prison cell
strip away mobility
carve into flesh
but they could never win
that's the beauty of justice
it knows no sympathy
for oppression

A Closing Bow

I.

standing on the subway
a Black dancer, no more than 20
smile beaming off the doors
politely asks a white man
no less than 50
to please stride to the side

it is 2 p.m. on a Tuesday
congestion is light
seats are still available
but needless to say
where the white man is standing
a bit of room is required
for the dance routine

the white man doesn't reply
stays stoic, face unseen
by the rest of the car

the young dancer
graciously asks him once more
to make room for the extravaganza
that's about to take place
tosses in a joke for good measure
in keeping with affable displays
since the last subway stop

the older man remains grim
and curtly replies *no*

unshaken
the dancer carries on
navigates
       around
white obstruction
tries to find room
for his feet
in this crowded path

a microcosm
on a Tuesday afternoon
blocks paths
refuses to budge
stays curt and grim
from the attitudinal
to the structural

there is no statistic for these
manifestations of racism
no comprehensive study

where is the physical violence
the handcuffs, the bloodied baton
the bruises, the marks of the hate crime?
where is the video, the perfectly placed scene
the media would seek to discredit?

II.

kids I went to high school with
go on about the good deeds
of cops

the media focuses on
the bad apples, they say

> *a Black body is pulverized*
> *every 28 hours*
> *the barrel is rotten*
> I reply

why is it always about
Black people? the skeptic inquires

> *why was slavery always*
> *about Black people*
> *Jim Crow*
> *separate water fountains*
> *lynchings, Emmett Till*
> *and Barack Obama's*
> *birth certificate?*

> *why are white people*
> *never the victims*
> *of these crimes*
> I respond

we are past that stuff
the colorblind apologist
implores

as if the dancer's skin color
on the subway didn't transform
that white man into an
immovable object

he didn't have to say the N word
it was on the tip of his eyeballs
beaming through the car
post-race ace cards
in society's back pocket

the dancer just swiveled on by
collecting contributions
overflowing in a hat
stopped in front of the man
to let his earnings
dangle for a moment
as if a finishing touch
on the production

and in a closing bow
the subway doors
stretched open
like a curtain call

and with all the grace
and confidence
in his performance
the dancer disappeared
into the crowd
on the platform

Layover in Palestine

I.

on a balcony in Bethlehem
Abu Iyad spoke slowly
in Arabıc
as if a typewriter
were catching every
letter and intonation

his wrinkled fingers
grappled with a coffee cup
contemplative and precise
contours of the Nakba
mapped into the history
of his face

we stood in front of
chopped-down olive trees
a stump-encrusted hillside
stripped of its ferriliry
       barbed wire
choking the periphery

banned from land
by occupation forces
who kicked down
his door and abducted
him and his son

II.

feeling like a tourist
outside my own skin
passing, never present
wanting to touch everything
I came in contact with
in case my palms never
pressed down on
this earth again

every trip like a last goodbye
entry never guaranteed
visa never guaranteed
nothing ever guaranteed

what is the purpose of your visit?
where was your father born?
come with me
put that down
take that off
spread your legs
you understand that
this is for security?

you can go
    words I thought
    I would never hear again
a kid with peach fuzz
and a grimace
chest puffed
and trigger-finger itchy
    what hollowed drones
    humans become

got through and felt lucky
got through and felt ashamed
got through and felt ashamed
that I felt lucky
the empire's passport
burning a hole
in my back pocket

just want to sit and be present
feel what it is like to be home
without someone pulling
on my shoulder
taking me away

Palestine stays
under a microscope
    always communal
never ours

it is exhausting
struggle, liberation
a campaign, a Facebook post
an infographic, constantly searching
for the right words to say
the right message to bring
when all I want is to feel
present in this space
take in this breath
and exist here
if only
for a moment

Credits

My deepest appreciation goes to the editors of the following
publications, who first showcased versions of poems
featured in this collection:

"Until It Isn't." Originally published in *Letters for Palestine*,
edited by Vijay Prashad (Verso, 2015)

"Refuse," "Peace Process," and "Normalize This!" Originally
published in *Wasafiri* 80 (Winter 2014)